PreFabNow

PreFabNow

COLLINS | DESIGN

An Imprint of HarperCollins*Publishers*

James Grayson Trulove

and Ray Cha

PreFabNow
Copyright 2007 © by COLLINS DESIGN and James Grayson Trulove

HarperCollins books may be purchased for educational, business, or sales promotional use.
For information, please write: Special Markets Department, HarperCollins Publishers,
10 East 53rd Street, New York, NY 10022.

First published in 2007 by:
Collins Design
An Imprint of HarperCollins*Publishers*
10 East 53rd Street
New York, NY 10022
Tel: (212) 207-7000
Fax: (212) 207-7654
collinsdesign@harpercollins.com
www.harpercollins.com

Distributed throughout the world by:
HarperCollins*Publishers*
10 East 53rd Street
New York, NY 10022
Fax: (212) 207-7654

Packaged by:
Grayson Publishing, LLC
James G. Trulove, Publisher
1250 28th Street NW
Washington, DC 20007
Tel: (202).337.1380
jtrulove@aol.com

Design and Art Direction by: Agnieszka Stachowicz

Library of Congress Cataloging-in-Publication Data

Trulove, James Grayson.
  Prefab now / James Grayson Trulove.
      p. cm.
  ISBN-13: 978-0-06-114988-7 (hardcover)
  ISBN-10: 0-06-114988-8 (hardcover)
  1. Prefabricated houses. 2. Architecture, Domestic. I. Title.

  NA7145.T78 2007
  721'.04497--dc22

                        2007007130

ISBN: 978-0-06-114988-7
ISBN-10: 0-06-114988-8

Manufactured in Korea
First printing, 2007
1 2 3 4 5 6 7 8 9 / 08 07 06 05

Contents

MOD 3, by Studio 804 incorporates a number of eco-friendly materials and practices.

5 3 4

Foreword

A NEW GENERATION OF ARCHITECTS HAVE EMBRACED PREFABRICATION, bringing an end to the era when the baggage-ridden term invoked the image of a double-wide trailer home. On the contrary, this international group of designers is exploring new potentials for using factory-built architecture in unexpected ways. By reinventing prefab, they are addressing the needs of the present day, be it for self-expression, environmental sustainability, or social concerns.

Today, prefab architecture spans the wide spectrum of architecture. Architects LOT-EK and FutureShack, with their signature repurposing of shipping containers, make bold design and philosophical statements. Rippled metal sidings propel their prefabrication intentions to the forefront of their designs. On the other hand, the modular formats of Resolution 4: Architecture and Alchemy Architects' weeHouses cleverly disguise their houses' prefabricated beginnings. Their custom factory-built modules are combined to make each of their houses strikingly unique. Anyone seeing these finished projects would not immediately recognize them as prefab, if at all.

Developments in prefabricated architecture have progressed in step with advances in sustainable architecture. This relationship comes on many fronts. Reuse plays a major overlapping role here, from shipping containers to Jennifer Siegal's ingenious commercial-trailer home addition. Beyond reuse, architects have seized the opportunity to integrate sustainable design concepts starting at the initial beginnings of their design phase. These innovations include new eco-friendly building materials, as implemented in Studio 804's Mod 2 and Mod 3 and CH14.

Factory-built mass production of houses can lead designers in unexpected directions. For example, Sean Godsell Architects capitalizes on the benefits of mass production with FutureShack. Here, this house uses recycled shipping containers to create structures that can be easily produced, stored, and shipped. Needing only twenty-four hours to be fully erected, the Future Shack was envisioned as a response to emergency housing needs, such as natural disasters.

An exciting genre is developing at a rapid pace. Each year, new firms eager to push the bounds of prefabricated homes join the ranks of established prefab designers. Their designs will challenge how we think about building houses and will offer innovative choices for those fortunate people contemplating the construction of a new home.

Projects

Mountain Retreat

FOR ENTERTAINING AND GUESTS

ARCHITECT **RESOLUTION: 4 ARCHITECTURE**

LOCATION **UPSTATE NEW YORK**

PHOTOGRAPHY **FLOTO + WARNER**

A LIFTED-BAR MODULE AND A TWO-STORY BAR MODULE FORM THE basis for this 1,800-square-foot weekend home in the Catskills. The client wanted a home that would allow for guests and for indoor and outdoor entertaining. Within its 1,800 square feet are two bedrooms and two bathrooms and a loft-like living space.

By combining the lifted bar and the two-story bar, maximum floor space is achieved on a minimal footprint.

The first floor accommodates a sitting room, a bedroom with bath, and a carport. Upstairs, looking out on forested views, is the open living, dining, and kitchen area surrounded by a large deck for entertaining. The kitchen separates the master bedroom and bath from the common areas.

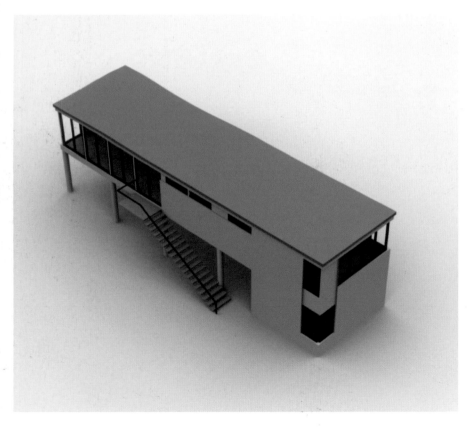

LEFT: A model of the lifted bar. By lifting the living space and the two bedrooms in the house to the second level, the owners enjoyed better views. This topology is well suited to heavy-rain climates, because living spaces are above the flood level. A carport is on the ground floor as is a home office or additional bedroom.
ABOVE: A model of the two-story bar. This topology allows maximum interior spaces on a minimal footprint, making it suitable for situations where there is limited buildable space on the site. The outdoor terrace, elevated above the terrain, provides a generous space for outdoor entertaining.
RIGHT: A view of the carport with stairs leading to the second-floor terrace that surrounds the living area.

See page 172 for a full description of Modern Modular construction

14 Mountain Retreat

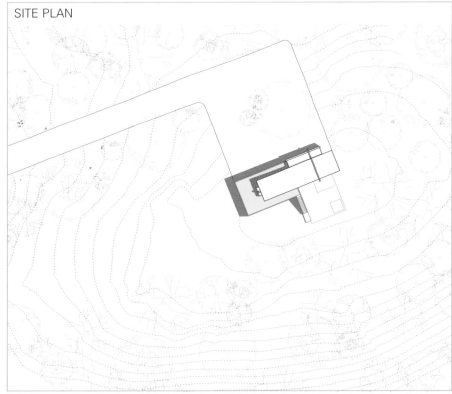

SITE PLAN

CLOCKWISE FROM LEFT: Construction views showing the factory where the house is being prepared for trucking to the site. Prefabricated bars are being lifted into place. Once the bars have been assembled on-site, exterior sheathing is applied.
FOLLOWING PAGES: A view of the entry to the completed house.

FIRST FLOOR PLAN

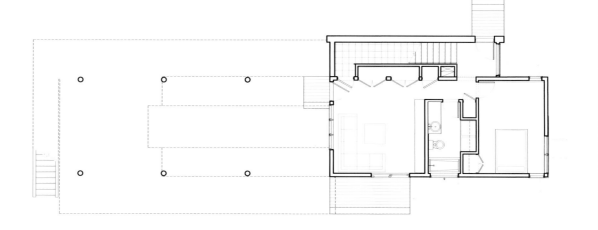

SECOND FLOOR PLAN

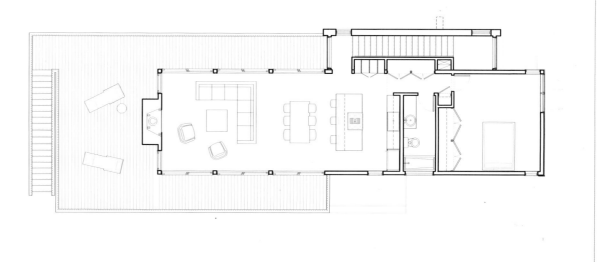

LEFT AND ABOVE: The 1,800-square-foot house is a synthesis of the lifted-bar and the two-story bar. The ground level features a carport and a bedroom, while the main living quarters are on the second floor. An exterior staircase connects the two levels. There is also an interior staircase at the entry.

ABOVE: A view along the second floor terrace that wraps around the living, dining, and kitchen areas. Shown here at the end of the terrace is the wall enclosing the interior staircase leading from the entry below.

RIGHT: Clerestory windows and operable sliding glass doors bathe the dining and living area in natural light while providing bird's-eye views of the surrounding forest.

ABOVE: A view of the kitchen from the dining area.

RIGHT: To the left of the kitchen is the door to the interior staircase that leads to the lower-level entry.

ABOVE AND RIGHT: Views of the living area.

LEFT AND ABOVE: The butterfly roof allows the master bedroom to enjoy additional light from clerestory windows.

LEFT AND ABOVE: The exterior is sheathed in long-lasting and low-maintenance horizontal cedar board and cementitious panels.

Cedar House

ARCHITECT **HUDSON ARCHITECTS**

LOCATION **UNITED KINGDOM**

PHOTOGRAPHY **STEVEN TOWNSEND**

NESTLED IN THE ENGLISH COUNTRYSIDE, THIS HOME UNTILIZES off-site construction that simplified the building process without compromising the architecture of the house. Designed for a photographer and his family, the 3,450-square-foot house consists of two bedrooms, a guest room/dark room, and a gallery/studio with a separate loading area for large canvases and prints. Given the rural location, it was important that the design be sensitive to its surroundings and blend comfortably with the local agricultural landscape. The result is a modest, traditionally styled home, simple in form and evocative of a functional farm building.

The surprise is that underneath the 15,000 untreated cedar shingles are prefabricated timber-panel floors, walls, and roofing, which allowed the entire building to be erected in just one week. Inside, the architects achieve complex and spacious interiors from a prefabricated system. Thanks to a lightweight roof structure, roof beams became unnecessary; the result is soaring ceilings and seamless open-plan spaces. This also permits large openings, even across corners, without the need for additional structural reinforcement.

The final design incorporates a large, cantilevered corner window that frames views of the river from the living room and about 25 feet of glazed doors that extend the living room out to a raised deck on the west side. Positioned on a north-south axis, the dwelling makes the most of the morning and afternoon sun. The kitchen faces east and the living room deck and entrance space looks west overlooking a planned orchard.

LEFT AND RIGHT: The simple structure blends quietly into the rural landscape. The aluminum-frame windows, large expanses of glass, and unadorned lines give the home a decidedly contemporary feeling.

FLOOR PLAN

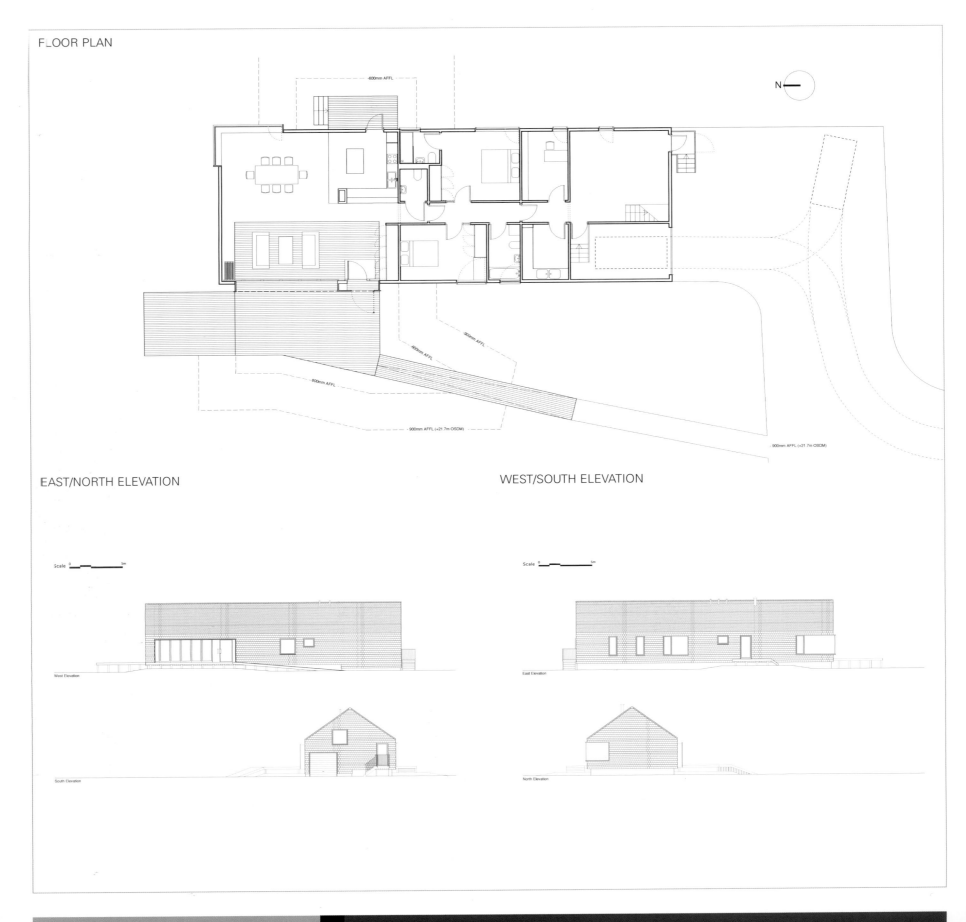

N

-600mm AFFL

900mm AFFL

-600mm AFFL

-600mm AFFL

- 900mm AFFL (+21.7m OSDM)

- 900mm AFFL (+21.7m OSDM)

EAST/NORTH ELEVATION

WEST/SOUTH ELEVATION

Scale 0   5m

Scale 0   5m

West Elevation

East Elevation

South Elevation

North Elevation

32 Cedar House

RIGHT: The open sliding doors reveal the expansive living space that spills out to the deck.

RIGHT: A view of the rear entry and garage.

BELOW AND RIGHT: Since a lightweight roof structure made structural beams unnecessary, the interior features soaring ceilings and seamless open-plan spaces, and large windows, even across corners.
FOLLOWING PAGES: Exterior view at dusk.

Bay House

WATERSIDE PREFAB

ARCHITECT **RESOLUTION: 4 ARCHITECTURE**

LOCATION **MARYLAND**

PHOTOGRAPHY **MATTHEW GIRARD**

BAY HOUSE IS A BLUR BETWEEN THE THREE-BAR BRIDGE AND the two-bar slip topologies for this waterfront site. The 2,500-square-foot home has a master suite, two studies, and 2.5 baths.

The two-bar slip is anchored by a central living space with large windows providing views in every direction, important for a site with splendid water and forest views. Two separate bedroom wings can accommodate a large family. The three-bar bridge model creates an optimum division of space by forming a bridge connection between three modular living units.

For Bay House, the master bedroom and bath are located on the ground level along with a separate study. The first floor is an open plan with the living-dining-kitchen area; a large outdoor deck wraps around this area. On the second floor is another study that opens onto a large deck with an outdoor fireplace. There is a family room on this level with its own outdoor deck as well.

LEFT: The main entry to the house is reached via a raised bridge that leads to the first-floor living area.

RIGHT: The rear of the house, which faces the water, has multiple outdoor decks. See page 172 for a full description of Modern Modular construction

SITE PLAN

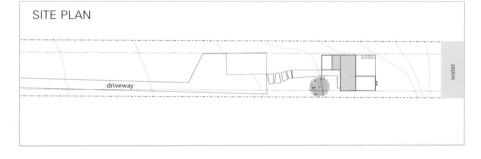

driveway

water

CLOCKWISE FROM LEFT: One of the modules being assembled in the factory; a view of the foundation; and the crane lifting a module at the site.

BASEMENT FLOOR PLAN

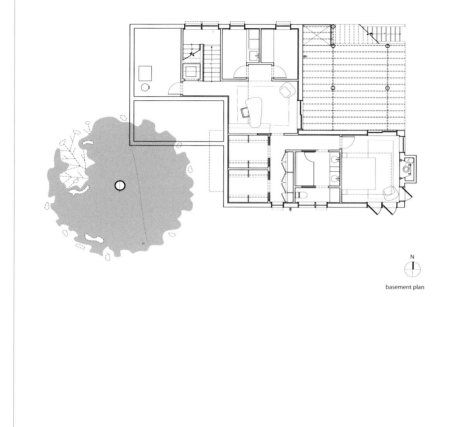

basement plan

MODEL

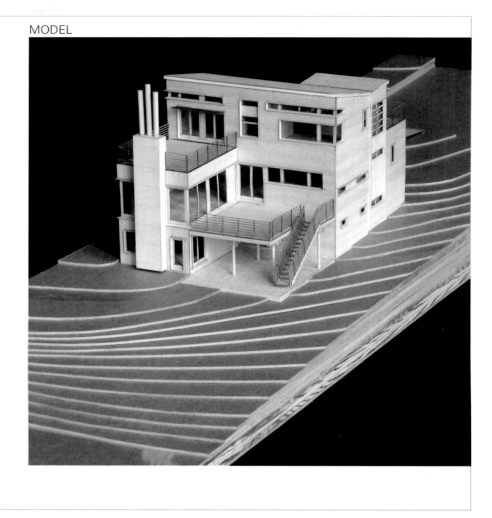

FIRST FLOOR PLAN

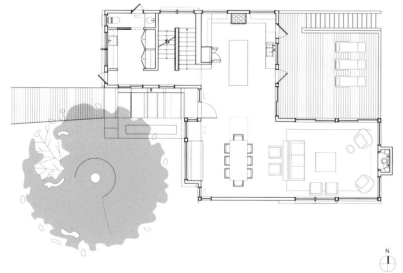

first floor plan

SECOND FLOOR PLAN

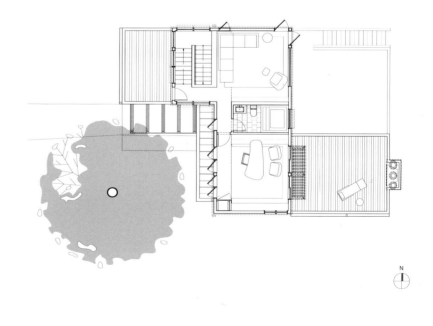

LEFT: The first-floor entry.
RIGHT: A view of the entry to the third-floor study from the adjoining deck.

ABOVE: A view of the dining area on the main level.
RIGHT: The living room on the main level.

ABOVE: The entry at dusk.
RIGHT: The second-floor deck with its fireplace and a view of the
water beyond.

Portable House

HERE TODAY, GONE TOMORROW

ARCHITECT **OFFICE OF MOBILE DESIGN**

LOCATION **CALIFORNIA**

PHOTOGRAPHY **BENNY CHAN, UNDINE PRÖHL**

THE PORTABLE HOUSE COMBINES TWO OF THE MOST DESIRABLE features of a prefabricated home: flexibility and portability. Its 12-by-60-foot steel frame structure can be trucked to the building site and set on a permanent foundation or one designed for a temporary siting before it is moved to another location to accommodate a new users' needs. Once in place, the exterior is clad with a combination of metal siding and translucent polycarbonate panels that serve as windows, eliminating the need for curtains and shades. Both materials are low-maintenance and low-cost and can be installed quickly.

On the interior, the sloping roof provides generous, high ceilings in the living area, then tapers back to a more intimate height in the sleeping quarters at the rear of the building. The central kitchen and bath core divides the living and sleeping spaces. A variety of sustainable floor and wall materials are used to finish the interior. Windows are positioned to provide ample passive cooling; radiant panels are used for heating. Fixtures include a Boffi kitchen and bathroom and an iPort sound system.

Whether temporarily situated on an urban lot or in an open landscape for emergency use, or positioned for a lengthier stay, the Portable House can accommodate a wide range of needs and functions.

LEFT AND RIGHT: Translucent polycarbonate panels are used for windows, providing ample light and ventilation as well as privacy. The Portable House is shown on a temporary foundation on an urban site.

FLOOR PLAN

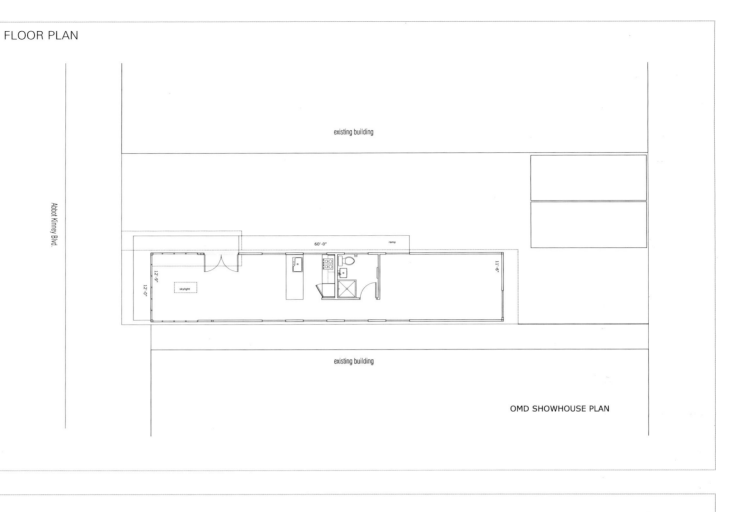

existing building

Abbot Kinney Blvd.

60'-0"

ramp

12'-0"

12'-9"

skylight

11'-6"

existing building

OMD SHOWHOUSE PLAN

LEFT: The exterior is clad in long-lasting metal siding attached to a preassembled steel frame.
FOLLOWING PAGES: The living and the sleeping / study area.

PREVIOUS PAGES AND LEFT: The Portable House is equipped with a living area and an office that could also serve as a bedroom. The spaces are divided by a central core that features an open kitchen and a bathroom. The floors are bamboo, a sustainable hardwood.

Shinohara Residence

AT HOME WITH NATURE

ARCHITECT **ANDERSON ANDERSON**

LOCATION **JAPAN**

PHOTOGRAPHY **COURTESY ANDERSON ANDERSON**

BELOW AND RIGHT: While each house uses standard prefabricated components, they are assembled to give each house a custom look and feeling.

THIS IS A PROTOTYPE HOME DESIGNED AS ONE OF A RELATED series of semi-custom, site-adapted houses for a developer in Japan. The all-wood construction consists primarily of 2-by-6-foot framing systems, used in conjunction with engineered wood roof structures. Each house uses repetitively prefabricated construction components that were assembled in Portland, Oregon. These components—along with windows, doors, cabinets, and hardware—were shipped from the U.S. to Japan in four containers to a nearby port and then trucked a short distance to the building site, a terraced hillside overlooking the city of Tsuruga, the surrounding mountains, and the Sea of Japan

Because the tight lot is flanked on either side by neighbors, the architects chose to create a U-shaped design, attaching the modules in such as way as to create a courtyard with major rooms facing onto it.

As this was a demonstration house, it was designed to incorporate a variety of roof shapes, from curved to flat, as well as window configurations so that the prospective buyer of one of these homes could visualize the range of choices available.

Inside, an open loft-like space with high ceilings and floor-to-ceiling windows makes the otherwise compact home appear more spacious.

FLOOR PLAN

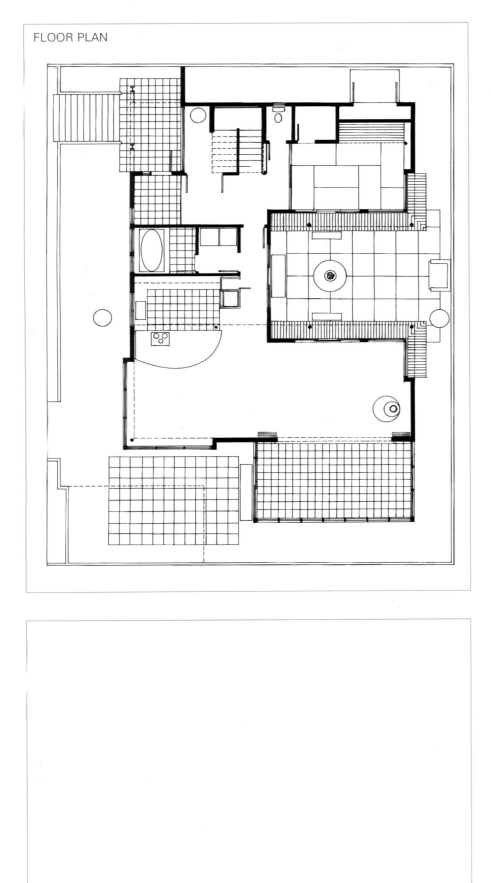

ELEVATIONS

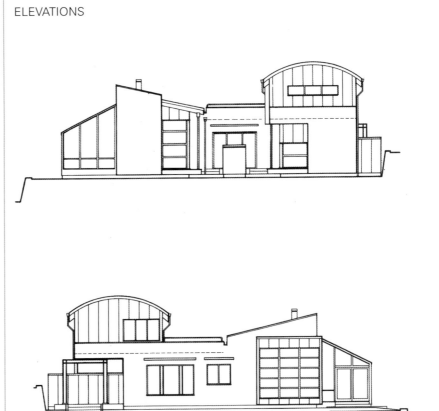

ABOVE LEFT: Prefabricated components are assembled on-site.
ABOVE: Generous use of windows takes advantage of panoramic city,
water, and mountain views. The ceiling reveals the custom-laminated
wood beams supporting the roof. The wooden-framed windows
were assembled in the United States and shipped to the site in Japan
for installation.

Country Retreat

SOPHISTICATED LIVING IN ROLLING HILLS

ARCHITECT **RESOLUTION: 4 ARCHITECTURE**

LOCATION **VIRGINIA**

PHOTOGRAPHY **STEPHEN WAUDBY,
RESOLUTION: 4 ARCHITECTURE**

THIS 2,600-SQUARE-FOOT HOUSE IS A MODIFIED VERSION OF RESOLUTION: 4 Architecture's two-bar L topology, where communal areas are on the lower level and private areas are on the upper level. With three full-sized bathrooms, a large master suite, and a flowing living-dining-kitchen area, the house makes a perfect country retreat. It provides both privacy, thanks to the site and layout, and ample entertaining space, particularly on a large outdoor terrace with a fireplace on the second level, above the living area. From this terrace, one has spectacular views of the Virginia countryside. Entertainment possibilities are further enhanced by an expansive ground-level stone courtyard with swimming pool. Low-maintenance horizontal cedar siding, with cement-board accents, adds a feeling of warmth to this carefree country home.

The entry court is flanked on one side by the house and on another by a matching two-car garage with frosted-glass doors set in aluminum frames.

LEFT AND RIGHT: A view of the west elevation with the entry and beyond. A bedroom is located in the extension with a terrace above; the second-floor media room looks onto the terrace.
See page 172 for a full description of Modern Modular construction

LEFT, CLOCKWISE FROM TOP: The east; west; west entry detail.
RIGHT: View of the east from the living-area wing. The patio is shown under construction.

ABOVE: The entry.
RIGHT: A view of the entry and outdoor court with pool from the studio.

ABOVE: A view of the dining and living area from the stone court.
RIGHT: A view of the dining and living area from the kitchen.

LEFT, CLOCKWISE FROM TOP: The kitchen seen from the dining area; stair detail; stairs leading to the second-floor bedrooms and media room.
RIGHT: First-floor bathroom with a view of the staircase beyond.

ABOVE: The butterfly roof provides the master bedroom with additional sunlight from clerestory windows.
RIGHT: The master bathroom.

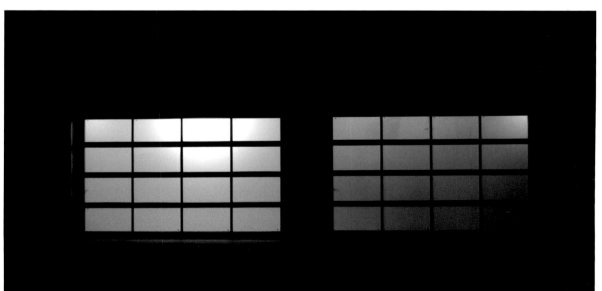

LEFT: The east.
ABOVE: The garage becomes a lantern at night with translucent doors that glow when backlit.

Cantilever House

ARCHITECT **ANDERSON ANDERSON**

LOCATION **WASHINGTON**

PHOTOGRAPHY **COURTESY ANDERSON ANDERSON**

THE DESIGN OF THIS 2,000-SQUARE-FOOT HOUSE INCORPORATES A low-cost, strong, manufactured building system that is easily adaptable to specific sites and differing home owner needs. It combines two common, standardized, mass-produced building elements—a prefabricated steel structural frame and structural insulated panels for exterior walls, the roof, and the floors. The design is easily adaptable to difficult site conditions such as the steep hillside shown here, since the modular steel frame structure can span between supporting columns or foundation walls and can cantilever up to 32 feet at the ends of the building. This minimizes the need to disrupt the natural topography and vegetation, and reduces expensive, on-site foundation work.

The modular system can accommodate a variety of accessory elements, including exterior decks and stairs, window boxes, sunscreens, and solar water heating or electrical generation panels. Such flexibility allows the owners to undertake additional customization over time, attaching accessory elements from many manufacturers without the need for custom attachment systems or costly modifications to the primary structure.

Although the materials and methods of construction were chosen for efficiency and affordability, the underlying design principles guiding the development of the system have the larger goals of producing affordable, high-quality homes that offer variety, adaptability, convertibility, strength, simplicity, spatial richness, and optimized access to views and light.

LEFT AND RIGHT: The modular steel frame design permits the living room and deck to soar over the landscape.

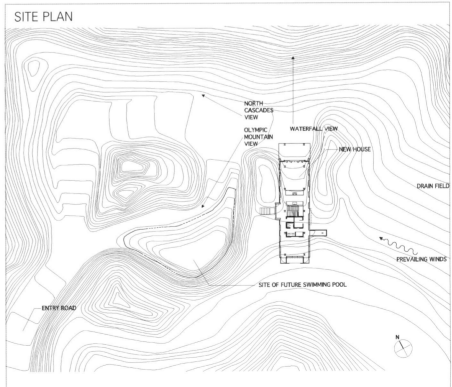

SITE PLAN

NORTH
CASCADES
VIEW

OLYMPIC
MOUNTAIN
VIEW

WATERFALL VIEW

NEW HOUSE

DRAIN FIELD

PREVAILING WINDS

SITE OF FUTURE SWIMMING POOL

ENTRY ROAD

N

UPPER LEVEL PLAN

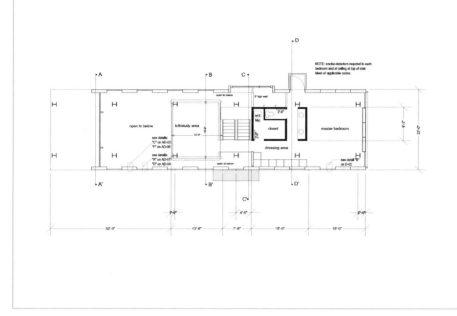

MAIN LEVEL PLAN

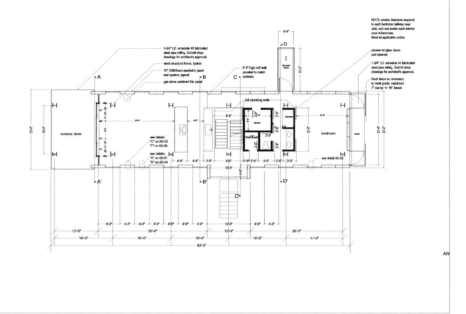

GROUND LEVEL PLAN

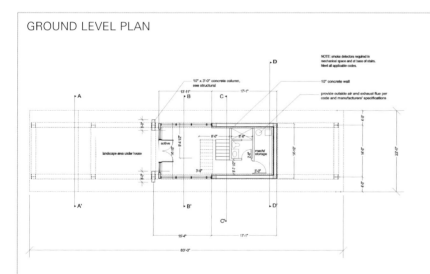

LEFT: In addition to providing great flexibility for placement and configuration of the foundation, the self-contained structural system is independent of the building enclosure and interior walls, allowing for equal flexibility in window placement and in the positioning and later modification of interior walls. RIGHT: The architects used an insulated aluminum storefront door and window system by Traco Manufacturing.

LEFT AND ABOVE: Since there are no load-bearing walls inside the house, the architects can customize the living space to suit the needs of the owners. The rich woods used here are in sharp contrast to the cool steel-and-cement board structural components and sheathing.

Chameleon House

TOWERING ABOVE THE LAKE

ARCHITECT **ANDERSON ANDERSON**

LOCATION **MICHIGAN**

PHOTOGRAPHY **COURTESY OF ANDERSON ANDERSON**

THE 1,650-SQUARE-FOOT CHAMELEON HOUSE SITS ABOVE A CHERRY orchard on a hill with a spectacular westward view of Lake Michigan and the surrounding agricultural landscape. The small, ground-floor footprint of the building reduces the cost of this expensive-to-construct area of the house and allows the foundation to step up the site following the slope of the hill.

In order to keep costs and on-site labor to a minimum, structural insulated panels (SIP) were used to construct the exterior walls and roof. The house was then sheathed in galvanized sheet metal. A two-story prefabricated steel frame on the lake side structurally allows for a double-height window wall and open loft-like spaces within the main living area. To help mask the scale, the building is wrapped in a skirting wall of recycled translucent polyethylene slats; these stand two feet out from the galvanized cladding on aluminum frames that serve also as window-washing platforms and emergency exit ladders.

Despite its development from off-the-shelf components, the house is carefully integrated into the rolling topography of its site, peering out to westward views of Lake Michigan and the surrounding agricultural landscape. Due to the slope of the site, the family enters at the third level, then descends to the children's bedrooms and bath or climbs to the main living spaces that look out over orchards to Lake Michigan.

LEFT AND RIGHT: The ever-changing appearance of the house and its ability to mirror the surroundings earned it the nickname "Chameleon House." The double skin creates a microclimate and thermal differential around the structure, creating a rippling mirage updraft that in the summer emits steaming condensation and in the winter drips melting icicles.

ABOVE: A view of the galvanized-steel siding being applied during construction.

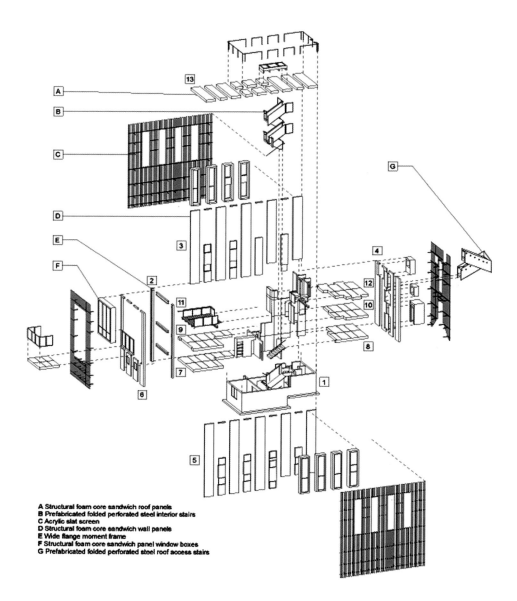

A Structural foam core sandwich roof panels
B Prefabricated folded perforated steel interior stairs
C Acrylic slat screen
D Structural foam core sandwich wall panels
E Wide flange moment frame
F Structural foam core sandwich panel window boxes
G Prefabricated folded perforated steel roof access stairs

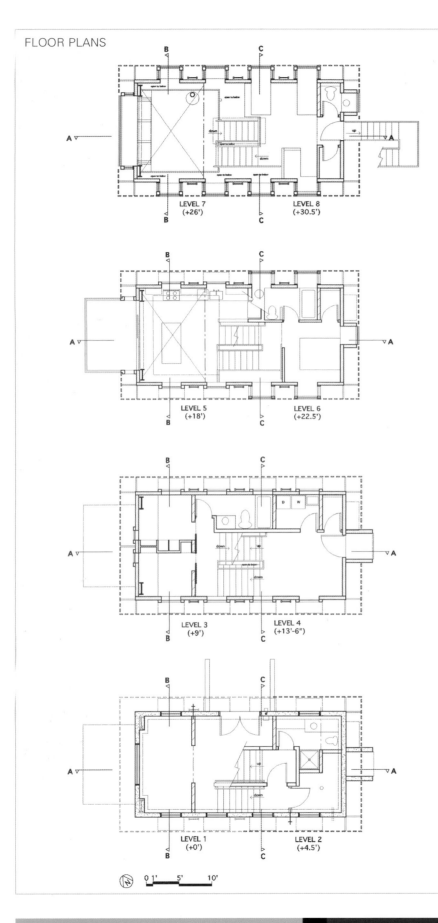

LEVEL 7
(+26')

LEVEL 8
(+30.5')

LEVEL 5
(+18')

LEVEL 6
(+22.5')

LEVEL 3
(+9')

LEVEL 4
(+13'-6")

LEVEL 1
(+0')

LEVEL 2
(+4.5')

0 1'   5'   10'

LEFT: Floor plans and models of the structure.
ABOVE: The exterior steel frame provides additional structural support for the large windows. The translucent polyethylene slats serve to visually minimize the mass of the building.

ABOVE: A view of the entry from the living area.
RIGHT: The tower design was chosen so that the owners would have views of Lake Michigan over the treetops.

LEFT: Stairs connect the nine levels of the house.
ABOVE: A generous balcony extends from the living area.
FOLLOWING PAGES: The house blends with its
snow-covered environment.

Red Cabin

TUG BOAT ON THE HILL

ARCHITECT **ALCHEMY ARCHITECTS**

LOCATION **MINNESOTA**

PHOTOGRAPHY **GEOFFREY WARNER**

A MODEST 750 SQUARE FEET IN SIZE, THIS WEEHOUSE IS CONFIGURED from one Solitaire module with one rooftop Companion module containing a bedroom that gives onto a deck. The stairway leading to the second bedroom was built on-site. The first-floor module contains a galley kitchen, an open dining-living area, and a bedroom and bath. The floors are maple laminate.

The rough-sawn siding, which was painted red, was chosen to mimic the wood cabins found in the area and to evoke the image of a tugboat sitting atop the hill. At the time of construction, the total cost for the house was less than $100,000.

BELOW AND RIGHT: With interior space limited, large decks on the roof and ground level expand the living and entertaining spaces. In order to preserve maximum usable interior space, the stairway to the second-floor bedroom and deck was placed outside.

FIRST FLOOR PLAN

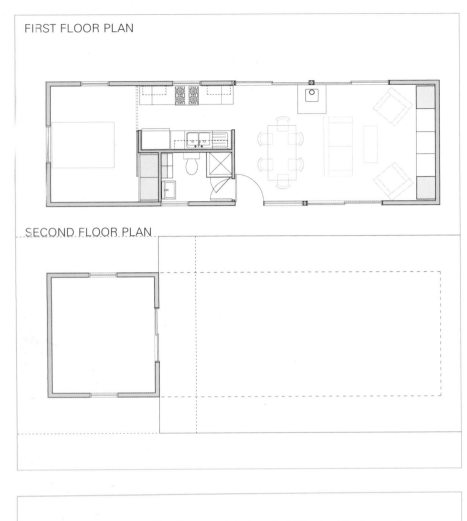

SECOND FLOOR PLAN

RIGHT: Although the first-floor module is only 14 feet wide, large glass sliding doors on either side of the living-dining area visually expand the space to the outside landscape.

ABOVE: Naturally stained maple-laminate floors and birch cabinetry and a complementary neutral palette of colors contribute to the spacious feeling of the living area.
RIGHT: A view of the galley kitchen with the master bedroom beyond.

KitHAUS K1

EXTRUDED TO SUIT YOUR NEEDS

ARCHITECTS **TOM SANDONATO, MARTIN WEHMANN**

LOCATION **CALIFORNIA**

PHOTOGRAPHY **NOLEN NIU**

THE KITHAUS CONSISTS OF MODERNIST MODULES THAT ARE assembled using a patented, extruded-aluminum frame and clamping system that accommodates a variety of designs and building types—from a vacation home to a standalone home office to a guest cottage. The all-aluminum 389-square-foot construction is impervious to the normal burdens of home ownership, including rust, termites, and mold; and it never needs painting. An existing kitHAUS can be expanded down the road, should the owner require additional space.

All assembly is done on-site from factory-supplied materials that are precut and predrilled. The kitHAUS is designed to be constructed on a raised foundation so that utilities can be run through the floor. Wall panels utilize an insulated foam-strand board sandwich, while the windows, doors, and sub-floors are energy-efficient. The client has the option of cladding the exterior in zinculume or ipe wood.

According to the architects, a 17-by-17-foot kitHAUS can be constructed in days without the use of ultra heavy construction equipment.

The modules come in two modernist styles, K1, which has a butterfly roof, and K2, which is equipped with a flat roof. The two models can be used separately, or they can be combined.

LEFT AND RIGHT: This 17-by-17-foot module, with glazing and an extensive deck, provides just under 300 square feet of living space. Additional modules may be attached at the time of construction, or later, as the owner requires.

SECTION

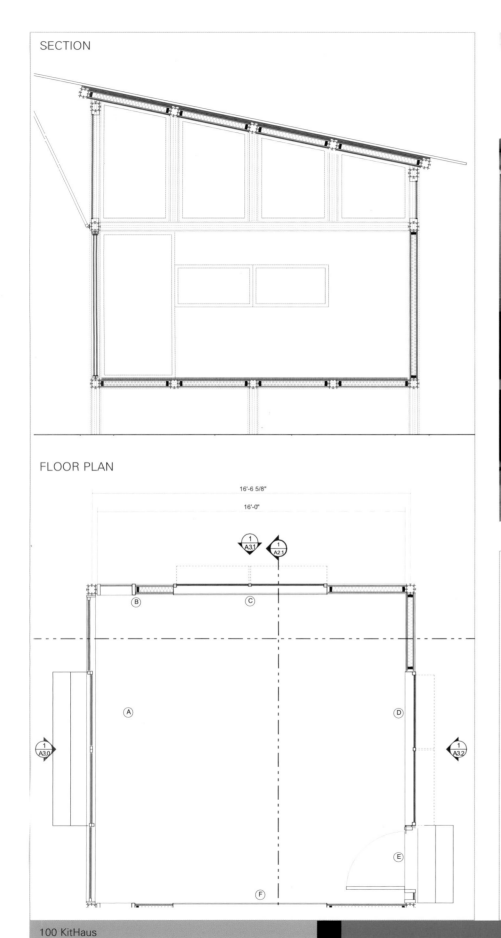

FLOOR PLAN

16'-6 5/8"

16'-0"

ABOVE AND RIGHT: Exterior sheathing consists of either zinculume or ipe wood, or a combination of the two. Windows and doors are framed in aluminum.

LEFT AND RIGHT: The extruded-aluminum frame is left exposed and becomes part of the modernist aesthetic of the kitHAUS. Entry is through sliding-glass doors.

ABOVE AND RIGHT: The ipe wood used on the exterior is used to create an accent wall in the living area. The floors are bamboo, a sustainable hardwood.

RIGHT: This module arrives at the site in the form of prefabricated materials. The architects say they can be assembled within days on a prepared foundation.
LEFT: The kitHAUS is available with a fully equipped bathroom.

X 1

A FIVE-STEP PROCESS

ARCHITECT **HIVE MODULAR**

LOCATION **MINNESOTA**

PHOTOGRAPHY **COURTESY OF HIVE MODULAR**

THIS MINNEAPOLIS-BASED FIRM HAS CREATED TWO TYPES OF modular homes. Each type includes a small, medium, and large version that can be ordered with either a flat or pitched roof, and with clean, modern or traditional siding and windows. The largest and most easily customized is the X-Line, with 2,300 finished square feet. On sloping lots, a finished, walkout basement can have a recreation room, a bath, and one bedroom.

The architects follow a five-step process when working with new clients. This includes acquiring a building site (the client's responsibility); creating a customized design from the modular options provided by the architects; engaging a local contractor—also the responsibility of the client—who, working with the contractor, will draw up cost estimates that include foundation and site preparation, the desired modules chosen, delivery and installation of the modules on the foundation, and on-site finishing work; obtaining necessary approvals and building permits; and finally, the actual construction of the home.

This modular home has a soaring central open space; a balcony with a study area overlooks this space. Large window openings provide dramatic vistas and flood the interior with natural light. A custom metal staircase in the foyer leads to second-floor bedrooms, bathrooms, and a laundry. Wood, stone, and tile flooring complement the clean design of the main floor; while carpeting on the upper level softens the ambience. The kitchen, the dining room buffet, and the master closet wardrobe have extensive built-in cabinetry.

The exterior is sheathed in maintenance-free fiber-cement and metal siding with aluminum-clad wooden windows. The house also features a non-modular three-car garage.

LEFT: A view of the living room from beneath the balcony.
RIGHT: The entry with an attached three-car garage.

LEFT AND ABOVE: In general, highway regulations limit the width of the modules to 16 feet and the length to 62 feet in most areas. Hive Modular homes are built with standard wood-framed construction materials, but they are strengthened and reinforced to withstand over-the-road travel. The modules feature 2-by-6-foot exterior walls with R-19 fiberglass batt insulation, engineered floor and roof trusses, R-44 roof insulation, three-quarter-inch glue and nailed-plywood subfloor, and glue-adhered gypsum wallboard. The vented flat roof system features factory-installed seamless rubber roofing.

FIRST FLOOR PLAN

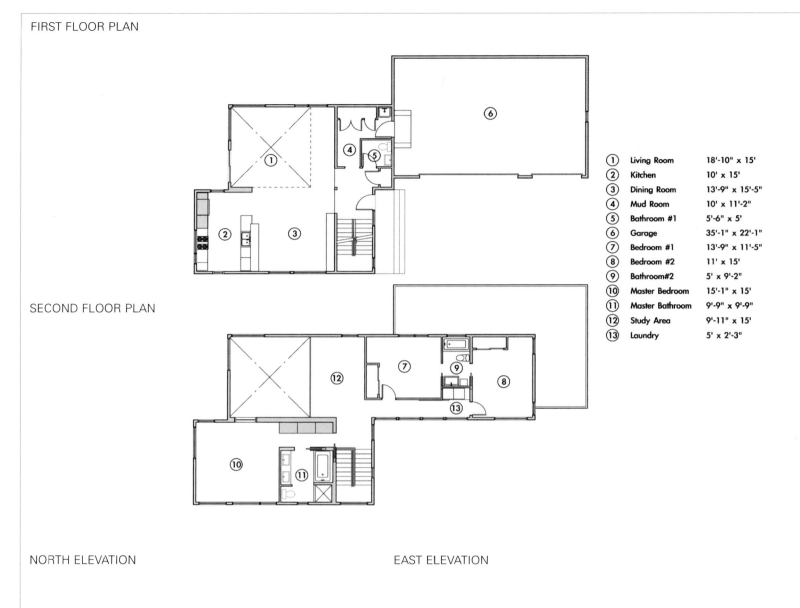

①	Living Room	18'-10" x 15'
②	Kitchen	10' x 15'
③	Dining Room	13'-9" x 15'-5"
④	Mud Room	10' x 11'-2"
⑤	Bathroom #1	5'-6" x 5'
⑥	Garage	35'-1" x 22'-1"
⑦	Bedroom #1	13'-9" x 11'-5"
⑧	Bedroom #2	11' x 15'
⑨	Bathroom#2	5' x 9'-2"
⑩	Master Bedroom	15'-1" x 15'
⑪	Master Bathroom	9'-9" x 9'-9"
⑫	Study Area	9'-11" x 15'
⑬	Laundry	5' x 2'-3"

SECOND FLOOR PLAN

NORTH ELEVATION

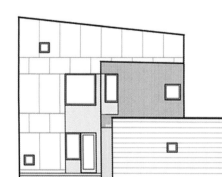

EAST ELEVATION

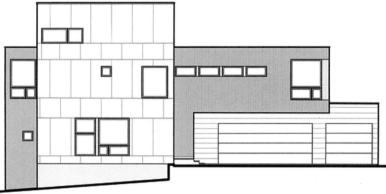

LEFT: A detail of the cement-fiber siding.

RIGHT: A detail of the entry showing the juxtaposition of the cement-fiber siding with the vertical metal siding and aluminum-clad windows—all maintenance-free.

ABOVE: The balcony with study area as seen from the living room.
ABOVE RIGHT: The cabinets and all plumbing fixtures are included in
the kitchen module. The owners are responsible for selecting and
installing appliances.

RIGHT: A view of the living area from the kitchen.
BELOW: The kitchen as seen from the dining area.

CH14

ADAPTS TO CHANGING NEEDS

ARCHITECT **CLEVER HOMES**

LOCATION **GEORGIA**

PHOTOGRAPHY **COLEEN DUFFLEY (INTERIOR)**

ERICA GEORGE DINES (EXTERIOR)

WITH 15 DIFFERENT PREFABRICATED HOME DESIGNS, THIS San Francisco Bay Area design-build firm constructs homes from coast to coast. This particular project was developed for *Better Homes and Gardens* magazine. Factory- engineered wall and roof panels were trucked to the site, and the home was assembled on its wooded site in about a week. These structural insulated panels are made from sustainably managed forest timbers. When assembled, the panels create a building envelope that offers substantial energy savings over traditional stick-built construction.

While this home has two bedrooms and two and a half baths, different configurations can add an additional bedroom and bath with total living space ranging from 1,500 to 2,500 square feet. There is also an optional two-car garage.

The siding on the house is made of low-maintenance concrete lap, designed to visually break up the facade and reinforce the horizontal lines of the home. The simple cedar screens lend pattern to the facade and gently shade the interior spaces without obscuring the views.

The bold horizontal lines of the roof—and the exterior as a whole—reinforce the effect of a streamlined Prairie Style home, its design driven by this early-twentieth-century school of modernist architecture.

LEFT AND RIGHT: The front porch is an important design element, creating a warm and welcoming spot for friends and neighbors to gather. The exterior is sheathed in low-maintenance concrete-lap siding.

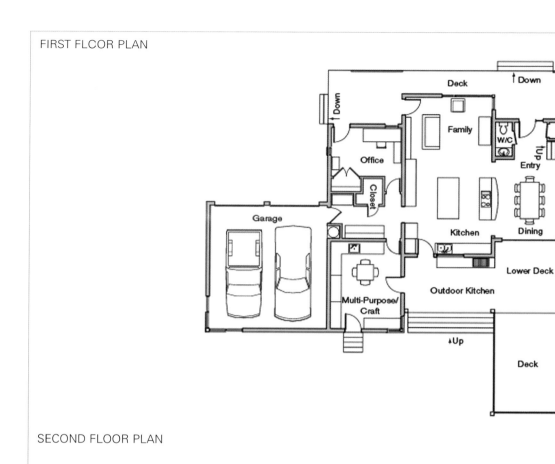

Deck

↑Down

↓Down

Family

W/C

Office

Up↑

Entry

Closet

Living

Garage

Kitchen

Dining

Lower Deck

Outdoor Kitchen

Multi-Purpose/
Craft

↓Up

Deck

SECOND FLOOR PLAN

Roof

Bedroom

↓Down

Bath

Office/Study

Bath

W D

Closet

Bedroom

Open

Closet

Master Suite

Roof

Roof

LEFT: The dining room.
FOLLOWING PAGES: A generous rear porch encloses an outdoor kitchen
and extends to a deck that embraces the surrounding woodland.

LEFT: The outdoor kitchen is located on the rear porch.
ABOVE: A master bedroom on the second floor.

ABOVE: The family room.
RIGHT: The formal living room has double-height ceilings.
FOLLOWING PAGES: The design of the house recalls Frank Lloyd Wright's
early-twentieth-century Prairie Style.

Siegal Residence

KEEP ON TRUCKING

ARCHITECT **OFFICE OF MOBILE DESIGN**

LOCATION **CALIFORNIA**

PHOTOGRAPHY **MARVIN RAND**

EXISTING HOMES CAN ALSO BENEFIT FROM A PREFAB ADDITION AS demonstrated by this project undertaken by the architect Jennifer Siegal to enlarge her own home in the eclectic Venice Beach neighborhood in southern California. Using the existing 800-square-foot home as a base, the architect removed walls and created a modern, open loft plan. To this, she added a 200-square-foot addition—an abandoned truck trailer that she purchased for $1,500 and had towed to the site, where it was lifted by crane onto a permanent concrete foundation.

The trailer's side-loading doors were replaced with floor-to-ceiling glass-and-steel doors, and a large glass-and-steel pivoting window was added. The back, loading end of the trailer was attached to the house and the connecting space holds a bath and laundry room. The trailer's original mahogany floors were sanded and reused.

LEFT AND RIGHT: The trailer addition at the rear of the house was placed perpendicular to the existing 1920s stucco bungalow. The elevated section of the trailer that originally accommodated the connection to a cab was concealed with a small, tiled spa pool. Images on this page show the trailer before installation of a pivoting window above the pool.

SOUTH ELEVATION

EAST/WEST SECTION

BELOW: The architect seamlessly blended the trailer addition with the existing house through the use of color and similar window treatments. In this recent image, the project is complete, a cozy addition in harmony with the neighborhood.

Texas Retreat

PREFAB ON THE PRAIRIE

ARCHITECT **ALCHEMY ARCHITECTS**

LOCATION **TEXAS**

PHOTOGRAPHY **JOSH CAPISTRANT**

ALCHEMY ARCHITECTS ARE RESPONSIBLE FOR A PREFABRICATION system that they refer to as the weeHouse. It is based on a factory-assembled module that can be configured to create a number of residential designs; they are readily adaptable to a variety of climates and terrain conditions. The homes are available as single-unit and self-contained Solitaries that may be combined with special-use Companions, which include living-dining-kitchen modules, bedroom-bath modules, and smaller staircase and utility modules. Each module is 14 feet wide and up to 56 feet long, the overall dimensions being determined by highway regulations.

The exterior can be customized according to type of siding, including wood, metal, or color; the type of foundation; and the choice of add-ons such as porches, decks, and roof overhangs. Interior options include the type of wood for floors and walls, the trim, the door hardware, the lighting, and the kitchen and bath finishes—much as one would expect when working with an architect to design a custom home.

The Marfa, Texas house is designed to serve as a simple retreat in this remote site outside the small arts colony of Marfa, Texas in West Texas. It is the first of three weeHouse modules planned for the site. Each module will arrive complete with an outdoor shed and a fully finished high-end interior and exterior, leaving only utility hookups, decks, and sun-shielding canopies to be installed on-site.

LEFT AND RIGHT: In keeping with the rugged site, the exterior is clad in rusted metal.

ABOVE AND RIGHT: The first module has been completed. A total of three are planned for the site.

FLOOR PLAN

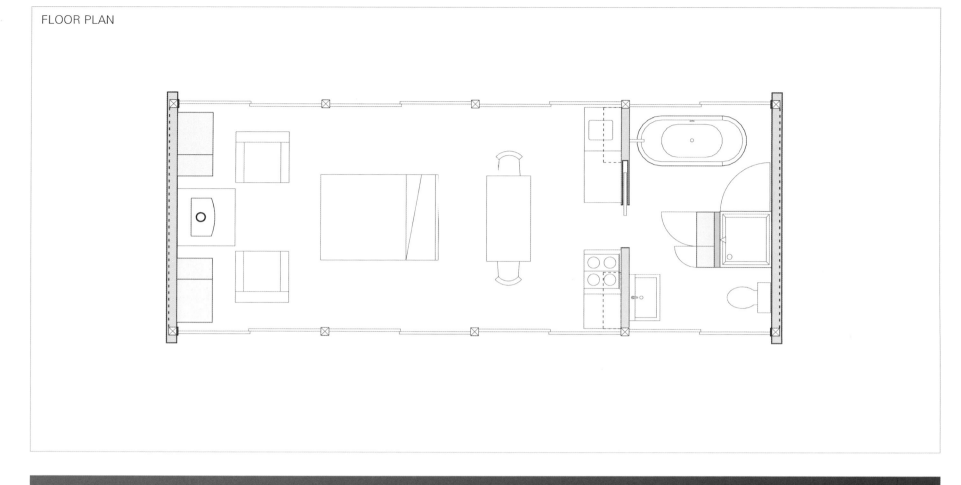

LEFT AND ABOVE: Custom interior finishes include wooden floors and walls, and a wood-burning stove for heat. At the other end is a fully equiped kitchen.

LEFT AND ABOVE: The weeHouse module is furnished with a spa like bathroom that offers views of the rugged Texas prairie.

Mod2 Shawnee

SUSTAINABLE AND AFFORDABLE

ARCHITECT **STUDIO 804**

LOCATION **KANSAS**

PHOTOGRAPHY **COURTESY OF STUDIO 804**

STUDIO 804 IS A DESIGN/BUILD PROGRAM AT THE UNIVERSITY OF Kansas School of Architecture and Urban Design that provides a broad range of architectural services, typically resulting in a new residence. Under the direction of Dan Rockhill, a noted architect himself, the students collaborate to bring a housing design to fruition that provides architectural solutions with an emphasis on affordable homes.

This dwelling was prefabricated in a warehouse fifty miles from the final site. It was built there as one complete house with seams that enable it to be separated into six 10-foot-wide pieces that would fit on flatbed trucks and under bridges.

Its destination: A foundation on a sloping site that accommodates a garage in the basement. The structure is entered via a drive that wraps around the house, starting from the street. The full basement also contains a third bedroom with a laundry room between it and the garage. The main, prefabricated living level is only 1,228 square feet with two bedrooms.

Horizontal, frosted channel glass, recycled from a museum expansion, provides soft, diffused light in the main living space. The glass is offset with recycled aluminum on the exterior face of the resulting recessed plane. The exterior is natural cypress. Inside, recycled maple flooring and a custom maple storage wall completes the material palette.

LEFT: The maple storage wall runs the length of the house from the living area to the master bedroom.
RIGHT: The house was constructed on a formerly trash-strewn lot where a home had burned to the ground many years ago.

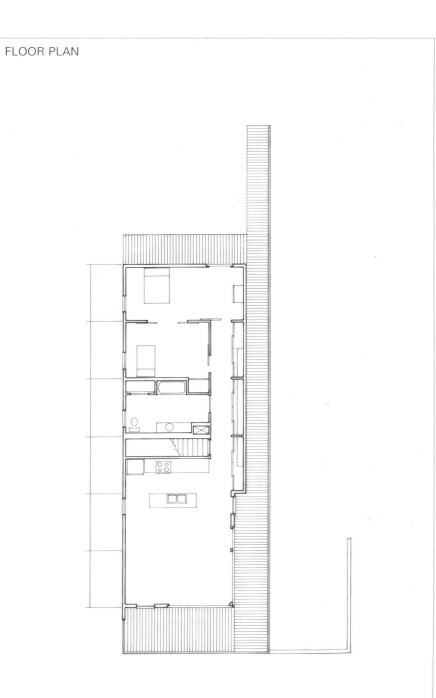

LEFT: A view of the house within the context of the existing neighborhood.

LEFT: The sloping site enabled the architect to place the garage and a third bedroom in the basement.
BELOW: At night, the frosted channel glass provides a sense of mystery.

SITE PLAN

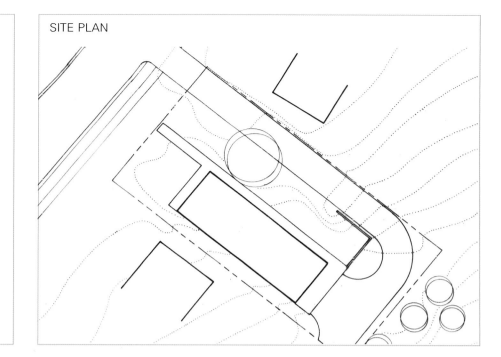

Mod3 Riverview

A VERY GREEN HOUSE

ARCHITECT **STUDIO 804**

LOCATION **KANSAS**

PHOTOGRAPHY **COURTESY STUDIO 804**

SUSTAINABILITY WAS A KEY CONSIDERATION FOR STUDIO 804 WHEN designing and building this modular home. Recycled cellulose insulates the wall, floor, and ceiling cavities—an exponentially improved method of insulation over the industry standard of fiberglass. Adjustable nighttime insulation over the large expanses of glass in the living spaces ensures thermal comfort. Highly efficient HVAC units ensure cost-effective heating and cooling. Exterior cladding of domestically grown Douglas fir was chosen in order to reduce fuel consumption associated with shipping materials from overseas. It is coated with a sustainable UV-water sealant. Use of extensive floor-to-ceiling windows provides dramatic views while insuring that interior spaces are flooded with light, reducing the need for artificial light.

A movable wall of shelves in a flexible space between the kitchen and bedroom can be slid on tracks from one end of the room to the other. It can nest tightly against one wall as a shelf unit, leaving the room open, or it can be moved out to form another bedroom, office, closet, or entertainment area.

A total of six factory-assembled modules make up the entire house. After they were attached to the foundation, the Douglas fir cladding was applied and HVAC and plumbing systems installed.

The finished product is a compact two-bedroom home on an elevated foundation with a large living area overlooking a protected deck. It was designed, built, and assembled over a five-month period.

ABOVE: A view toward the flex-space from the fully equipped kitchen.
RIGHT: A view of the cantilevered living area and secluded deck from the street.

LEFT: The horizontal Douglas fir siding enhances the long, horizontal profile of the building.
ABOVE: The entry.

MODEL

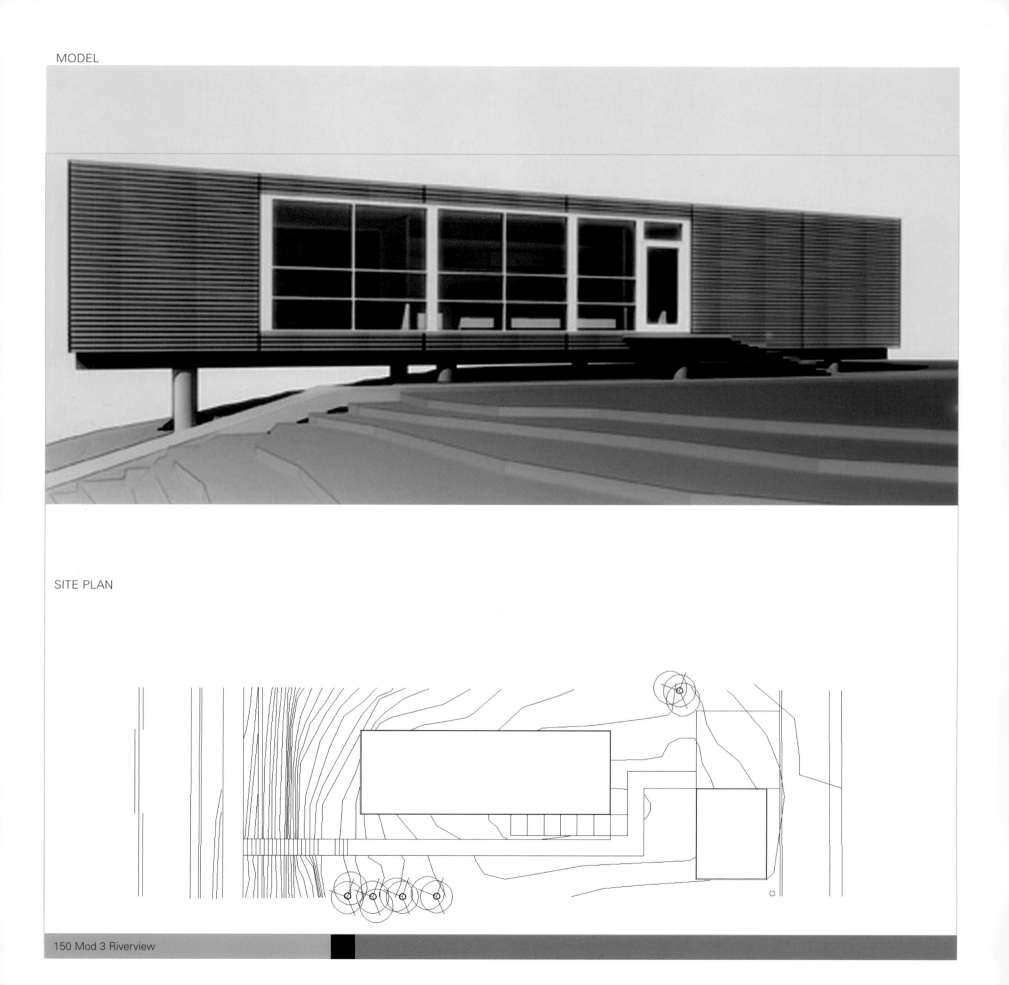

SITE PLAN

ABOVE: Oversized floor-to-ceiling windows provide the living area with abundant natural light. The living area is elevated above the sloping site, with a tree-top view of the downtown skyline.

LEFT: Tracks on the ceiling allow the bookcase to glide back and forth, to create different room configurations, depending on the need.
ABOVE: A view from the kitchen toward the living area and deck.

Container Home Kit

PROPOSED RECYCLED LIVING

ARCHITECT **LOT-EK**

USING RECYCLED SHIPPING CONTAINERS AS RESIDENCES HAS LONG fascinated the architects of LOT-EK, and they continue to explore ways to adapt these common industrial-like elements for domestic use.

The Container Home Kit utilizes multiple shipping containers to build modern, affordable homes. Branded CHK™ houses by the architects, the 40-foot-long shipping containers are joined and stacked to create housing configurations that can vary in size from approximately 1,000 to 3,000 square feet.

Each container is transformed into a living space by cutting sections from its corrugated metal walls. When joining the containers side by side, these cut outs expand the horizontal circulation along with the width of the container to create larger living spaces. The containers can be stacked to create double-height living rooms. Increasing the number of containers allows the house to expand from a one-bedroom home to ones with multiple bedrooms, as well as rooms for other uses.

Outside, additional containers can be used to configure a swimming pool, a pool house, a utility shed, and a car port. Totally recyclable, CHK™ houses can be disassembled and reassembled elsewhere as needed.

LEFT: Rendering shows how the kitchen and living space are created by combining shipping containers.

FLOOR PLAN

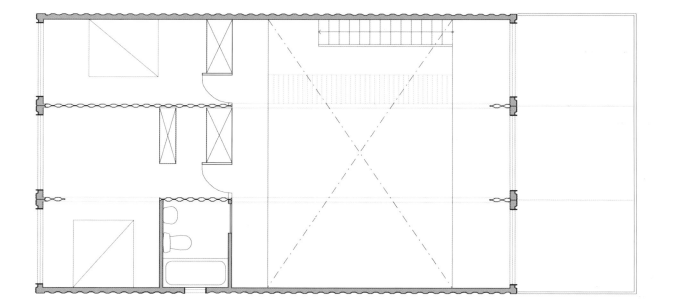

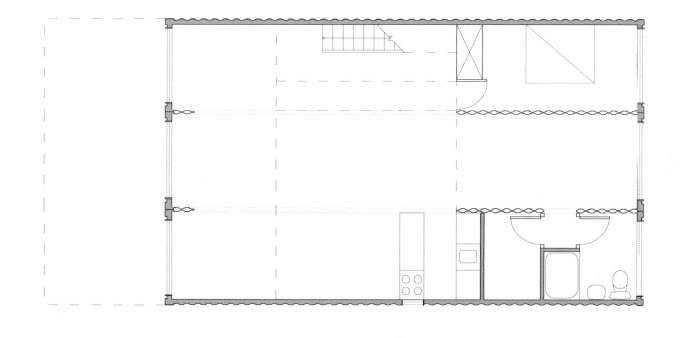

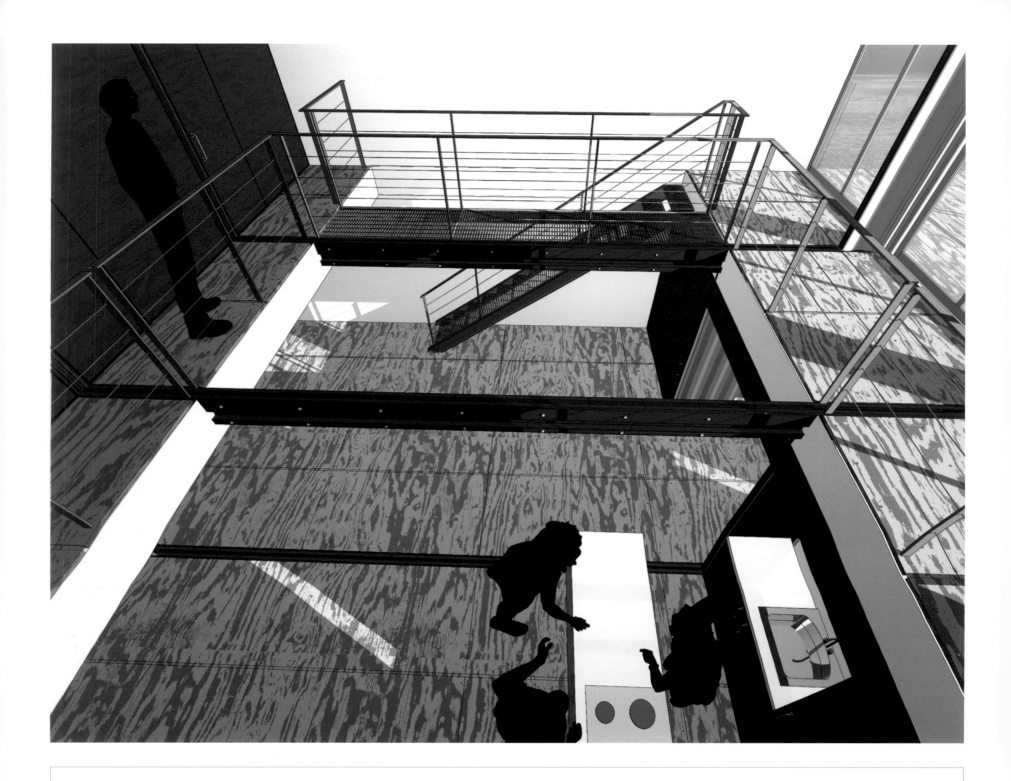

ABOVE: Portions of the containers are removed at either end to allow for windows and doors. The container's original plywood flooring remians in use.

RIGHT: Walkways around the edges of the containers on the upper level create circulation paths.

FutureShack

ARCHITECT **SEAN GODSELL**

LOCATION **AUSTRALIA**

PHOTOGRAPHY **EARL CARTER**

THE FUTURE SHACK IS DESIGNED TO BE A MASS-PRODUCED, relocatable home that can be used as emergency and relief housing. Recycled steel shipping containers form the main volume of the 160-square-foot building. A parasol roof is packed inside the container. When erected, the roof shades the container and provides protection from the weather. A pair of steel brackets fixed to the outside are also packed in the container. Inside the brackets are four legs that telescope out, allowing the module to be sited without the need for extensive site preparation.

Also packed within the container are water tanks, a solar power cell, a satellite receiver, a roof-access ladder, and a container-access ramp. The basic Future Shack is also equipped with thermal insulation to R4.0 and with vents for fresh air; it can be fitted with a small bathroom.

This home has a variety of applications—for example, shelter after natural disasters, temporary housing, third- world housing, and remote housing, among others. Because shipping containters such as those used for the Future Shack are available in most parts of the world, these temporary houses can be quickly fabricated and stockpiled for future emergency use.

Future Shack can be fully erected in 24 hours. Once it is no longer needed, it can be recycled as a shipping container.

LEFT, RIGHT, AND FOLLOWING PAGE: A fully erected Future Shack with the parasol roof unfurled. The roof is elevated to provide shade and air circulation above the container in hot climates.

ELEVATIONS

FLOOR PLAN

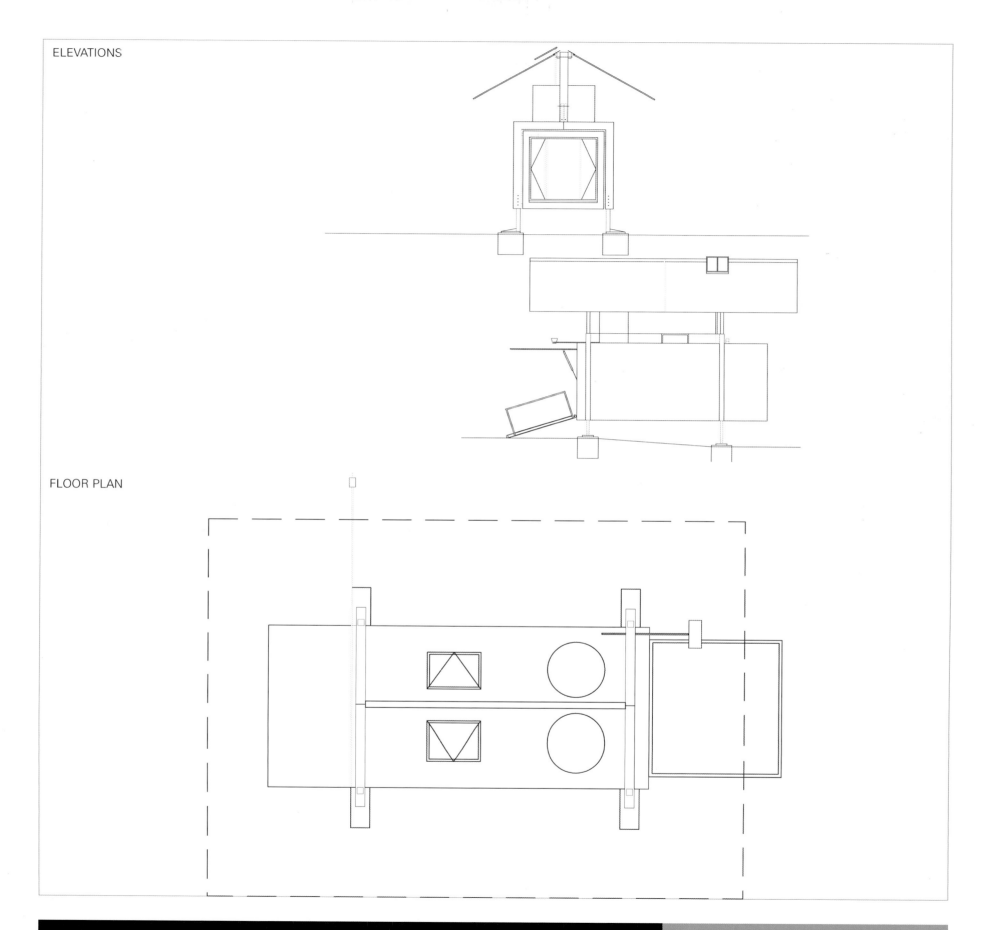

ABOVE: The compact interior is well vented and lined with plywood.
RIGHT: A simple bathroom has been added.

Mobile Dwelling Unit

ON THE MOVE

ARCHITECT **LOT-EK**

LOCATION **NEW YORK**

PHOTOGRAPHY **LOT-EK**

A BUILT EXAMPLE OF HOW LOT-EK HAS ADAPTED THE SHIPPING container for residential use is the Mobile Dwelling Unit (MDU). Here, one shipping container is transformed into a Mobile Dwelling Unit by making cuts in the metal walls of the container in order to create additional work and living spaces. The architects refer to these spaces as sub-volumes, which can be slid in and out as necessary. When the container is shipped to a new location, these sub-volumes are pushed inside the container, interlocking with each other and leaving the outer wall flush. When they are pushed out, they increase the square footage of the container by ten percent. The interior of the container and the sub-volumes are fabricated from plywood and plastic-coated plywood, including all fixtures and furnishings, creating a warm and inviting environment that is in sharp contrast to the industrial outer skin.

MDUs are for use wherever temporary housing is required or for the world traveler who wishes to keep his home and belongings with him at all times. The architects envision MDU vertical harbors in all major metropolitan areas around the globe that would accommodate the arrival and docking of these units.

For now, the MDU would make a perfect weekend retreat that can be easily secured when not in use.

RIGHT, TOP: Each niche addresses a particular need.
LEFT: A view of one sub-volume in use as a sleeping area.
RIGHT: The Mobile Dwelling Unit recalls a mid-century modern house.
Each sub-volume is a different size, depending on its function.

ABOVE: With the sub-volumes in the open position, the interior is visually engaging and spacious. Red, plastic-coated plywood and naturally finished plywood create a crisp, modern space.

FLOOR PLAN (with sub-volumes in the open position)

PANTRY
①

KITCHEN
②

SOFA
④

SINK
⑦

SHOWER

W.C.

NOOK
③

TV-DESK
⑤

BOOKCASE

CLOSET
⑥

BED
⑧

FLOOR PLAN (with sub-volumes in the closed position)

PANTRY
①

KITCHEN
②

NOOK
③

SOFA
④

TV-DESK
⑤

BOOKCASE

CLOSET
⑥

SHOWER

SINK
⑦

W.C.

BED
⑧

ABOVE: A complete bathroom is fitted into one sub-volume.
RIGHT: Another sub-volume contains a fully functional kitchen.

SECTION

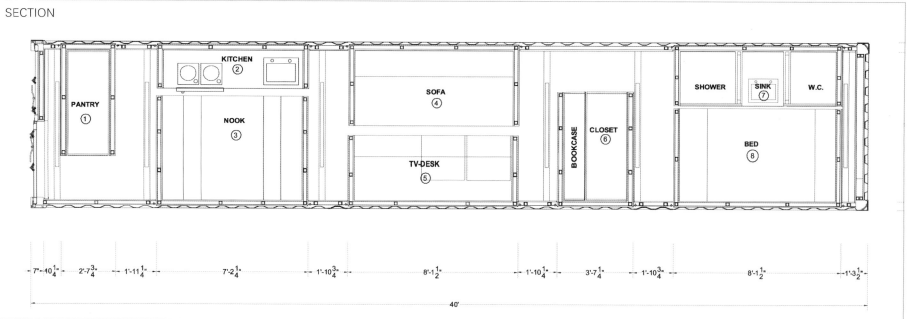

PANTRY ①

KITCHEN ②

NOOK ③

SOFA ④

TV-DESK ⑤

BOOKCASE

CLOSET ⑥

SHOWER

SINK ⑦

W.C.

BED ⑧

7"-40$\frac{1}{4}$" — 2'-7$\frac{3}{4}$" — 1'-11$\frac{1}{4}$" — 7'-2$\frac{1}{4}$" — 1'-10$\frac{3}{4}$" — 8'-1$\frac{1}{2}$" — 1'-10$\frac{1}{4}$" — 3'-7$\frac{1}{4}$" — 1'-10$\frac{3}{4}$" — 8'-1$\frac{1}{2}$" — 1'-3$\frac{1}{2}$"

40'

Modern Modular

PUSHING THE BOX

ARCHITECT **RESOLUTION: 4 ARCHITECTURE**

MODERN MODULAR WAS CONCEIVED BY RESOLUTION: 4 Architecture as a modern home topology to take advantage of the economical, environmental, and structural benefits of standard, proven modular construction techniques. According to the architects, advances in home construction technology have transformed the way in which houses are made, through factory assembly-derived construction techniques. The design of houses, they believe, has not changed significantly enough to take advantage of the possibilities of prefabrication and modular construction.

As a result, Modern Modular homes are designed with the flexibility to create a wide range of living solutions for differing home ownership requirements, from a simple weekend home to a full-time family residence. With standard modular living units as the starting point, the resulting houses are fully customized to meet the requirements of different locations and climates, and the specific needs of different households. Homes are easily expandable and transformed, allowing Modern Modular homes to grow and adapt to the changing needs of their residents.

Using the same customizable structure available in purchasing personal computers, the Modern Modular system transforms the traditional relationship between architect and client in home construction. Homeowners have limitless options for customization, based on the predetermined line of homes, and for additions to these standard types. The following three homes illustrate the broad range of homes that can be created using Resolution: 4 Architecture's approach to modular design.

RIGHT AND FOLLOWING PAGES: By choosing from the various modules above (communal use, private use, accessory use) an almost infinite variety of custom configurations can be created.

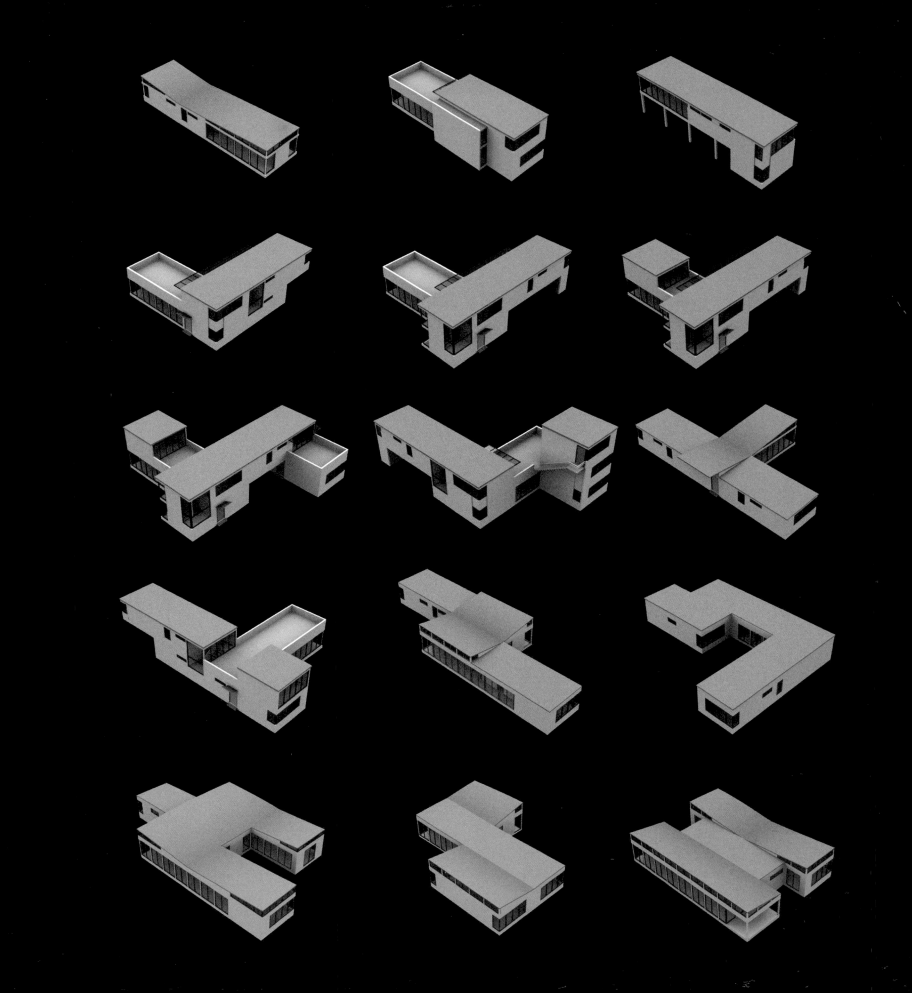

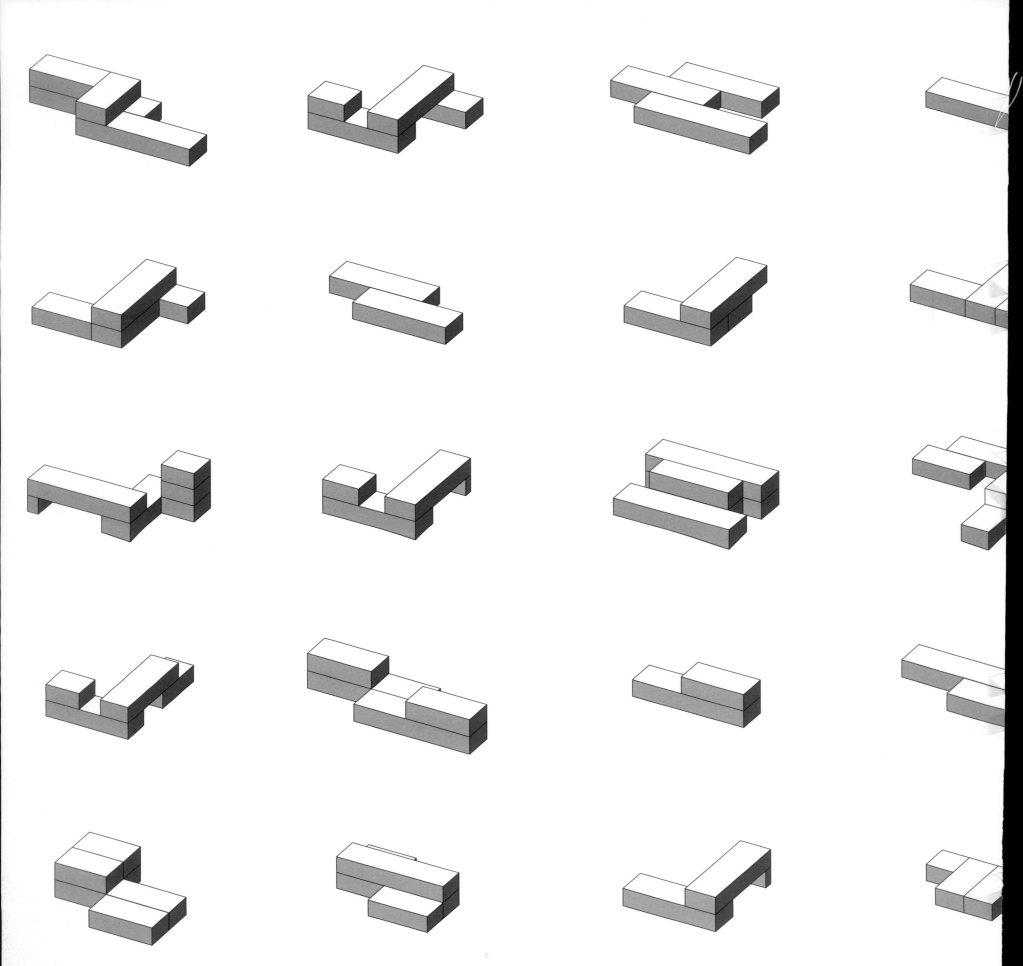

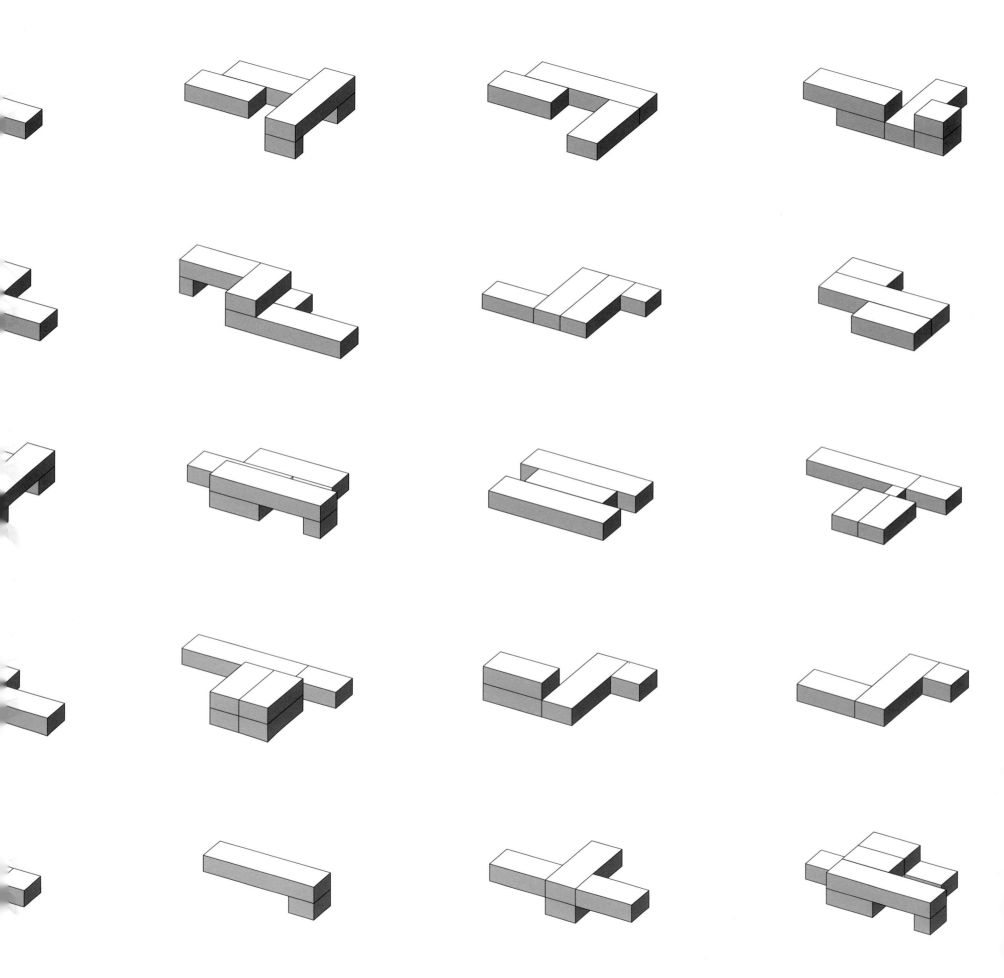

Pod

ARCHITECT **PREBUILT**

LOCATION **AUSTRALIA**

PHOTOGRAPHY **JOHN GOLLINGS**

PREBUILT IS AN AUSTRALIAN FIRM THAT OFFERS A WIDE RANGE OF prefab structures for vacation or full-time living. All are modestly priced, and each home is designed to be delivered in its entirety on a single truck direct from the factory.

Prebuilt homes are designed to have minimal impact on the environment. The homes are designed to be manufactured with little waste of materials. Should the owners decide to move to another part of the country, they can take their homes with them because they are designed to be transportable from one site to another.

Four models are presented here: the Pod, the Freedom, the Mod, and the Shed.

Shown here, the 1,000-square-foot Pod is centered around a core living-dining area. Separate pods may be added as here, for bedrooms or an office.

LEFT AND RIGHT: This Pod home consists of a central pod enclosing an open living-dining-kitchen area and a bathroom, with separate pods for a master bedroom suite connected via an exterior plank walkway and two additional bedrooms that are attached to the core.

FLOOR PLAN

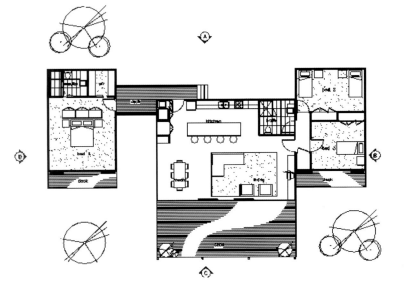

ELEVATION A

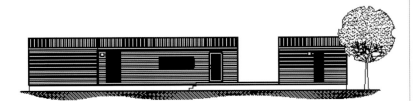

ELEVATION B

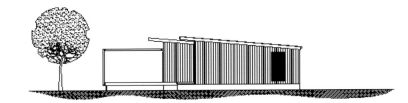

ELEVATION C

ELEVATION D

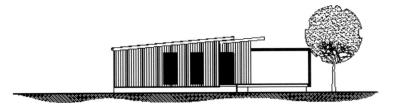

RIGHT: A view of the kitchen and living area in the central pod.

Freedom Home

RECALLING FARM BUILDINGS

ARCHITECT **PREBUILT**

LOCATION **AUSTRALIA**

PHOTOGRAPHY **JOHN GOLLINGS**

AT HOME IN THE AUSTRALIAN LANDSCAPE, PREBUILT'S FREEDOM home takes the iconic, corrugated Aussie shed and reinterprets it as a house for contemporary living. This design is perfect for anywhere, including steep slopes and compact sites. It is available in five sizes, ranging from two-bedroom, one-bathroom homes to three-bedroom-plus-study and two-bathroom homes. The design combines open-plan living and large windows for plentiful natural light.

BELOW AND RIGHT: This is a three-bedroom, two-bath model is 1,200 square feet, the largest of the Freedom houses. The metal siding recalls the farm buildings that dot Australia's landscapes. The corrugated cisterns capture rainwater.

GROUND FLOOR PLAN

MEZZANINE FLOOR PLAN

RIGHT: The open plan combines the living, dining, and kitchen areas into one large, open space. The cabinetry and bar are built in.

ELEVATION A

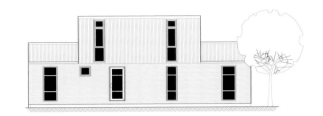

ELEVATION B

ELEVATION A

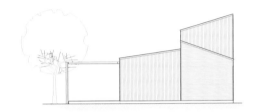

ELEVATION C

ELEVATION B

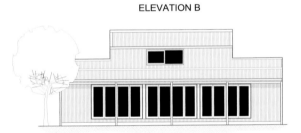

ELEVATION D

ABOVE AND RIGHT: The master bedroom and bath are located on the mezzanine level.
LEFT: Ground floor guest room.

Mod and Shed Houses

CONTEMPORARY AND TRADITIONAL

ARCHITECTS **PREBUILT, PLEYSIER PERKINS, COLLINS &TURNER**

LOCATION **AUSTRALIA**

PHOTOGRAPHYJOHN GOLLINGS

FLOOR PLANS(MOD) FLOOD SLICER GOLLINGS

THE MOD HOUSE (RIGHT) IS BASED ON A SYSTEM OF 5-BY-16-METER modules. Starting with a one-bedroom single-module home, the range extends to a triple-module home with four bedrooms and a study. Strikingly modern in appearance, the home has high ceilings and commercial-grade aluminum windows.

Prebuilt is currently working with Sydney-based Collins & Turner Architects in the development of the new Shed House range (below). Recalling the Australian woolshed vernacular, these modular units will be designed singly or combined.

FLOOR PLAN (MOD)

ELEVATION A

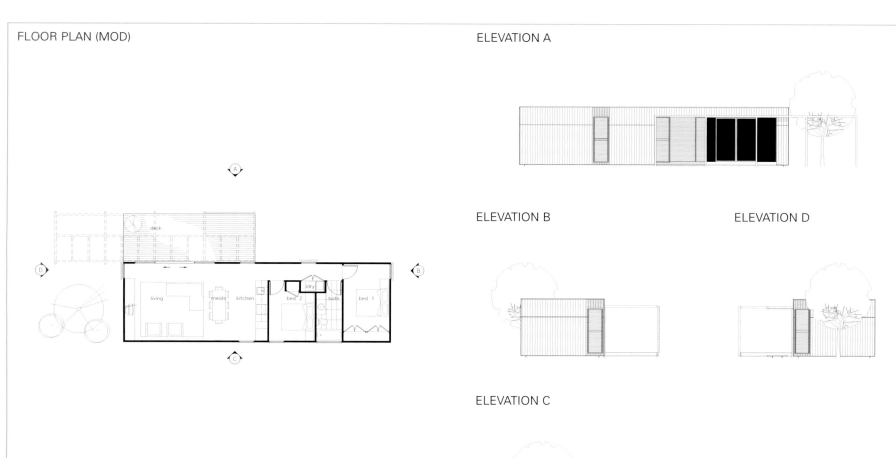

ELEVATION B

ELEVATION D

ELEVATION C

GROUND FLOOR PAN (DOUBLE SHEDS)

GROUND FLOOR PAN (SINGLE SHED)

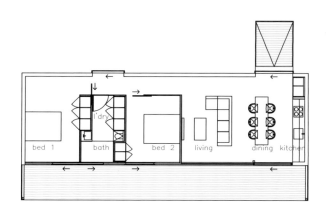

Directory

LOT-EK
55 Little West 12th Street, Top FL
New York, NY 10014
t: 1.212.255.9326
info@lot-ek.com
www.lot-ek.com

Resolution: 4 Architecture
150 West 28th Street, Suite 1902
New York, NY 10001
t: 1.212.675.9266
info@re4a.com
www.re4a.com

Alchemy
856 Raymond Avenue
Saint Paul, MN 55114
t: 1.651.647.6650
info@weehouses.com
www.weehouses.com

Anderson Anderson Architecture
83 Columbia Street, Suite 300
Seattle, WA 98104
t: 1.206.332.9500
90 Tehama Street
San Francisco, CA 94105
t: 1.415.243.9500
aaa@andersonanderson.com
www.andersonanderson.com

CleverHomes
665 Third Street, Suite 400
San Francisco, CA 94107
t: 1.415.344.0806
info@cleverhomes.net
www.cleverhomes.net

Sean Godsell Architects
49 Exhibition Street, Level 1
Melbourne Victoria 3000
Australia
t +61 3 9654 2677
godsell@netspace.net.au
www.seangodsell.com

Hive Modular
1330 Quincy Street NE, Suite 306
Minneapolis, MN 55413
t: 1.877.379.4382
info@hivemodular.com
www.hivemodular.com

Hudson Architects
49-59 Old Street
London EC1V 9HX
UK
t: +44 (0) 20 7490 3411
info@hudsonarchitects.co.uk
www.hudsonarchitects.co.uk

KitHAUS
15952 Strathern Street
Van Nuys, CA 91406
t: 1.310.889.7137
info@kithaus.com
www.kithaus.com

Prebuilt Pty Ltd
219 Colchester Road
Kilsyth Victoria 3137
Australia
t: +613 9761 5544
info@prebuilt.com.au
www.prebuilt.com.au

Jennifer Siegel
OMD, Corp
1725 Abbot Kinney Blvd
Venice, CA 90291
t: 1.310.439.1129
info@designmobile.com
www.designmobile.com

Studio 804
University of Kansas
School of Architecture and Urban Design
1465 Jayhawk Blvd
Lawrence, KS 66045
t: 1.785.864.4024
rockhill@ku.edu
www.studio804.com